LAFAYETTE

D0576488

SandCastle 1

The Alphabet

Kk

CONTRA COSTA COUNTY LIBRARY

Kelly Doudna

ABDO
Publishing Company

3 1901 03532 4674

Published by SandCastle™, an imprint of ABDO Publishing Company, 4940 Viking Drive, Edina, Minnesota 55435.

Copyright © 2000 by Abdo Consulting Group, Inc. International copyrights reserved in all countries. No part of this book may be reproduced in any form without written permission from the publisher. SandCastle™ is a trademark and logo of Abdo Publishing Company.

Printed in the United States.

Cover and interior photo credits: Comstock, Digital Stock, Eyewire Images, PhotoDisc

Library of Congress Cataloging-in-Publication Data

Doudna, Kelly, 1963-
    Kk / Kelly Doudna.
        p. cm. -- (The alphabet)
    Includes index.
    ISBN 1-57765-404-8
    1. Readers (Primary) [1. Alphabet.] I. Title.

PE1119 .D676 2000
428.1--dc21
[[E]]   00-028882

The SandCastle concept, content, and reading method have been reviewed and approved by a national advisory board including literacy specialists, librarians, elementary school teachers, early childhood education professionals, and parents.

Let Us Know

After reading the book, SandCastle would like you to tell us your stories about reading. What is your favorite page? Was there something hard that you needed help with? Share the ups and downs of learning to read. We want to hear from you! To get posted on the Abdo Publishing Company Web site, send us email at:

sandcastle@abdopub.com

About SandCastle™
Nonfiction books for the beginning reader

- Basic concepts of phonics are incorporated with integrated language methods of reading instruction. Most words are short, and phrases, letter sounds, and word sounds are repeated.

- Readability is determined by the number of words in each sentence, the number of characters in each word, and word lists based on curriculum frameworks.

- Full-color photography reinforces word meanings and concepts.

- "Words I Can Read" list at the end of each book teaches basic elements of grammar, helps the reader recognize the words in the text, and builds vocabulary.

- Reading levels are indicated by the number of flags on the castle.

Look for more SandCastle books in these three reading levels:

Level 1
(one flag)

Level 2
(two flags)

Level 3
(three flags)

Grades Pre-K to K
5 or fewer words per page

Grades K to 1
5 to 10 words per page

Grades 1 to 2
10 to 15 words per page

Karen has fun
making cookies.

Karly keeps talking.

Kelly has a cupcake.

Kim and Ken run.

Kent likes his kite.

Kendra rides a trike.

Kevin rides a bike.

Kay looks at a book.

What does Kayla
hold?

(kitten)

Words I Can Read

Nouns

A noun is a person, place, or thing

bike (BIKE) p. 17
book (BUK) p. 19
cookies (KUK-eez) p. 5
cupcake (KUP-kake) p. 9
fun (FUHN) p. 5
kite (KITE) p. 13
kitten (KIT-uhn) p. 21
trike (TRIKE) p. 15

Proper Nouns

A proper noun is the name
of a person, place, or thing

Karen (KAIR-in) p. 5
Karly (KAR-lee) p. 7
Kay (KAY) p. 19
Kayla (KAY-luh) p. 21

22

Verbs

A verb is an action or being word

More **Kk** Words

kangaroo

karate

key

koala bear

24